D1739251

The Outer Hunt for
Inner Success

The Outer Hunt for Inner Success
Gurney Allan

A way of finding purpose, fulfillment,
and the fullness of life

These contemplations came to me during times of fearful seeking and helped teach me how to move towards me.

Introduction

"You don't direct the soul. You feed it. Then the soul directs you."

Dallas Willard

Summary

The mind does not create happiness.
The mind does not create contentment.
The body does.
So don't use your mind
to problem solve your way
to happiness, contentment, joy, and peace.

Impossible.

Use your mind
to observe your body.
Watch what brings it delight.
And use your mind, to follow your heart.
And then use yourself
to offer your mind courage
if it doesn't like
where the body wants to go.

2022ish

"Until you make the unconscious conscious, it will rule
your life and you will call it fate."

Carl Jung

The Walk

I walked the world.
Trying to discover how I could bring it value.
Hurting myself.
Sacrificing myself.
Trying to do good.
Trying to create, achieve.
So people would think I was good.
So I would feel good.
So I could tell myself I'm useful.

My Mind

My mind.
It wants to create.
To take credit.
Not to receive.
And what it creates,
doesn't really resonate.
Especially with me.

The Change

I worry I worry I worry.
bout having to work.
About not having my time.
I want my time.
I think if only I Have time,
I'll be happy.
But on days when I have all the time,

I worry I worry I worry.

So I know,
the change that needs to be made.
Is the internal world,
Not the external.

Want

I want to achieve.
I want to be great.
I want to help.
I want to be free.
I want to find the right thing
that I can pursue
and work hard at.
Free my time.
And leave an impact on this world.

And I've been willing
to sacrifice how I feel
 - my good feelings -
to be great.
And where I have gotten in that state?
Not far.

Arising

Sitting.
An arising.
Emotions.
Not trusting.
Not feeling.
Contracting.
Rudding.
Pain.
The teachings -
bad motions are bad.
Is it true?
Suppressing.
Sitting.
Accepting.

Accepting.
Accepting.
Accepting.
Smiling.

Compassion.

Measure

What have I become
What do I have to show for myself?
Why do I insist on measuring myself on my
accomplishments?

Goodness

Goodness gracious.
Will this feeling ever leave me?
The feeling that I need to do something.
That feeling that I need to accomplish.
It contracts my entire being.
Maybe I do a startup? Maybe write a book?
What can I do what can I do what can I do what I do.
I do not want to feel this way.
Feeling like I have no value.
Just for being me.

Don't forget

I am great.
Everyone is wounded.
I love myself.
Offer everyone compassion.

Paredon

I wish I'd gone.
To ol' Paredon.
But that day has gone.
And a new path dawns.

So now, I know.
I've missed a show.
And my tears show
for something I do not know.

It's weird to lose
something you have never known.
If I could choose,
There I'd have flown.

What was there?
I do not know.
Why do I care?
Oh I wish I could know.

Good night, sweet Paredon.
Good night, what could have been.
Even though I never knew ya,
I hope someone did.

Lack

I'm too caught up with the act,
that's just a fact.
I've just been looking to achieve,
even if it makes me grieve.
It's no longer time to focus on what I lack

Mantra

All there is this moment.
All you get to do whatever you want with it.
It is a gift.
It is fun to anticipate the various moments
life may throw at you.

For nothing of the external world can change your
internal experience of this moment.

You have everything you need.
And can get everything you want.

What a joy. How lucky.

Witness

It might become behooving,
to stop focusing on grimacing.
If that thought you start losing,
You can enjoy witnessing
the act of your own becoming.

Heaven

Are you going to do?
To get to the next thing?
To get out of this thing?
Or are you here?
Are you intentionally feeling the moment?
Letting it enlive you?
Move through you?
Be you.
That's what heaven is.

An evening

What am I doing with my life?
If not creating something of value?
If I'm not helping people?

You're not here to be a helper.

Not

You're not great
if you don't do something
that is perceived exceptional.

That is what I learned.

What I was not told
is that
that is judging yourself
based on how an other judges you,
which is based on how society has told them to judge
society at large.

Be brave.
Be the judge of your own success.

Life

I love listening to people say,
"I love life."

Because as of late,
"I love life"
has a weird ring in me.
As if it's not registering.

It reminds me of what I have forgotten.
That I did love life.
And I know still do.

Somewhere -

The hard parts make it interesting.
Even they, are being given.
I'm smiling as I write this.

Let It Be

Plagued by desire.
Hurt by work.
Rolled over and busted.

I lie here
and relax.

Well, this is life.

So be it.

You, let go.
You can let go.
Let it happen.
And let it be.
You'll see.
Oh, you will see.

Overworking

If you act not from authenticity,
you're going to force yourself
to work frantically.
And is fun art going to come from that place?

Yet if you act authentically,
Discipline will come easily.
It still sometimes may not be fun.
But you'll be working from joy instead of need.

Consideration

Upon careful consideration,
I have but no choice to accept
that all the best things in my life
have come into of their own accord,
accompanied by minimal doing of my own.

And as such,
I have to realize that it would be foolish of me to
think I can single-handedly create what's best for me.

Feeling

Follow what feels good.
The more good you feel,
The more good will come to your life.
The more pain you follow,
The more pain will come to your life.

The more pain you avoid,
The more pain will come to you.
Feel the pain that is here.

The more you move in what is here,
The more good will come to you.
The more you feel what is here,
The quicker the pain will leave you.

Young

I go through life
in the same way I used to try to and give as a young man.
Rushed, contracted, forced, fast.
Trying so hard to please.
Not knowing
that less effort
gets better results.

Do Do

Part of me wants to do do do do.
When I do I can tell myself I've done stuff.
And when I've done stuff I can tell myself I'm satisfied.
I can tell myself that the day was well spent.
Feeling satisfied is what is truly desired.
So just feel satisfied.
Make that feeling contingent on loving, on being - not
doing.

Seeking

There is a difference
in how you pursue love and in how you pursue career
and art.
In love,
you pursue without worry.
You pursue without stress.
Without need.
Only with expectation.
That you deserve the best.
For you know, you do not need this love.
And you know you are perfectly happy
not having it.

Thoughts

I like playing with my thoughts.
Focusing on different sides of the same coin.
One moment I'll hate this.
And love that.
And the next I'll love this.
And hate that.
Oh, the pointlessness of it all.
I take leave to my garden.

Choice

First,
a series of values.
Everything is here.
I need nothing.
I deserve everything.
Love is to be spread.

People are not their personalities.
The world is trying to help you.
All you need to do is to
decide and receive.
Deciding what feels true to you
and finding the courage
to follow it and to accept it.

Achievement

The entirety of my being is hyper focused
on achieving a single goal I care not about.

Like some dog, yapping just to yap.

Dread

Oh gosh.
The dread.
The terrible, terrible thought that
I am here for nothing more than to just enjoy myself and
experience life.

Oh gosh.
I think it might be real.
All of us, children at large.

Integration

I hated, hated my job.
I was so embarrassed to tell people
what I did.
And I hated doing it.
I hated speaking about it.
I hated it.

But I told myself
that this was what I wanted.
And that I needed to swallow my ego.
And that the ego didn't matter.

In hindsight, I don't think I needed to fight my ego.
Following it blindly isn't ideal.
But ignoring it, it would seem isn't either.

If I had listened
and thought okay,
you don't like this?
What else might I do?
Well, I think I would have saved a bit of time.

Lurks

A great weight lurks over my body.
A great expectation.
Squeezing just hard enough
so that relaxation and joy
do not easily come in.

All

You could build a roof to protect yourself from pain.
But then you wouldn't be able to see the stars.
You can't prevent pain without stopping joy's reign.
So trust in all that you are.

Career

Letting go of trying.
Observing what I'm being.
A career becomes clear.

Path

Finally after much searching
and only after relinquishing,
letting go of some of the need to be externally valued,
a career path has appeared.
That lets me tell myself I'm helping.
That lets me tell myself I'm achieving.
But not in the way I expected.

But in a way that's integrated.
And relaxing.
And peaceful.
And exciting.
First and foremost, it's for me.

It's not business.
It's not art.
It's something that I never would have expected, and
simultaneously is something that's always been here.

Back to school I guess.
It'll take me years to get there.
I need money in the meantime.
I still want to do something. Create something.
I want a hobby or something to do and pursue..
        A great purpose.

2023ish

"Peace is your home, integrity is the way to it, and everything you long for will meet you there."

Martha Beck

Debt

What stress.
What stress fills me now.
20K in debt starting a new business..
And my contract has just been cut.

I tried to start my own thing.
I got my dream contract.
And now it is gone.

The anxiety is enough to cause
constant soreness in my jaw.

No clear path towards making money.
No clear path towards
not accumulating more debt.

Well.
The answer isn't in the future.
It's in the here and now.
And it's not going to come from a place of freaking out

Oh boy.

Art

It's quite surprising to me,
to realize that art can feel good.

I've realized that all the art I've been trying to do
hasn't felt good to me at all.

This is particularly surprising.
What reason is there to do art?
If not to feel good?
What was I trying to do?

Now, I love letting the world do.
And letting me flow in it.

Cup

It's funny what
being in nature,
having fun,
and filling up your cup
can do for business.

Spring

The Spring.
Good luck trying to find it.
It is a place that can only be found
By those not trying to look for it.
And trying to not try counts as trying

Purpose

You do not know why you are here.
I promise you there is a purpose.
You just don't know what it is.

Probably not much point in
worrying about not knowing what it is.
Trust there is one.

You're like a dog at the vet.
It's scary.
And seemingly pointless.
And hurts.
But you're there because it's helpful.
Even if you don't have the ability to reason why.

And that's all you get to know.

For now.

Turmoil

The internal turmoil comes
when what I force upon myself
is different than what is.
I think I should be happy right now.
But I am sad, sore, and tired.
And then I get annoyed
with myself for not being happy.
And thus I become less happy than I already am.

Mess

A room full of mess.
My mind on full roam.
But after a few deep breaths.
And a good place for things to rest.
My actions are my own.

Joy

Oh wow.
A silent home at night.
There's nothing better.
Than to lay on the ground
And write.

Cheese

Cheese! How delightful.
Never stops being tasty.
Never makes you full.

Dine

What have I become?
29 and not with money to dine.
You're figuring yourself out, hun.
Now isn't that fun.

Treasures

Perspectives, stillness, and nature...
The only treasures you can collect
that will bring you freedom.

Nothing

What is it?
That I would do today
if I needed nothing?
If I wasn't concerned about money, happiness, bettering,
or creating?
And I wasn't worried about opinions?
I would give.
And learn about the world.

Singing

Singing is interesting.
I'm singing in ways I never thought possible.
Nor in ways I think anybody ever thought possible for
me.
I mean I'm still not close to being good.
But I'm a lot better than I was.

I think a part of it was
that i had a story in my head
that other singers were inherently
on another level than me.
Which is true.
But I had it in my head that I had to try super hard
to be like them.
And that trying!
Trying to be on another level.
Trying to be something I'm not.
Took me away from my authenticity.
My trust of myself.
And what is art if not authentic?
What is expression if not authentic?
I had it all along.

Laughing

Not laughing much?
Empty your mind,
and the delight of everyday
you will suddenly find.

Reminder

Once again, I'll remind you.
It's hard to let it sink in.

You are not necessarily here to be happy.
You are not necessarily here to achieve.
You are not necessarily here to leave a mark.
You are not necessarily here to change others.

It's hard to say in words what you're here for.
But I would not say you're here
to not experience all that you are.

Balance

A step forward,
if you're not balanced,
is probably not forward at all.

Don't get lost in the lust for movement.

Stillness

What can be more productive
than finding stillness?
For only in stillness,
in balance,
in self love and acceptance,
does the path forward present itself.

Person

Giving up the somebody I'm not,
and focusing on the somebody I am,
it would suddenly seem I have not been raised at all
to be the someone I'm not.
And that I'm very uniquely molded
to be the best person I am.

Desire

Stillness.
Welcomes gratitude.
Gratitude.
Welcomes peace.
Peace.
Welcomes giving.
Giving.
Welcomes all you desire.

Source

I like the idea of source.
The idea makes me feel humble.
The idea makes me feel peace.
The idea makes me feel trust.
The idea makes me feel free.

Achievement

I told myself I love me this morning.
And thus have already achieved
what I normally spend an entire day
trying to do.

Life

Breathe and smile.
Smile and breath.
Breathe and smile and smile and breathe.
That's life baby.

Far

You'll never get
 to where you want to go
if you're afraid of not being there.
Allow yourself to be where you are.
Staying put Is how you go far.

Lies

Social media will have me believe
that I need to constantly be travelling to be happy.
What is life without travel travel travel fun?
And I'll impoverish myself to make that happen.
So I don't have to tell myself
that I'm not living my best life

But if I put down my phone for a while,
I realize that the backyard
opens my heart like no other.

Centering

A centering in myself
has found more understanding
than centering in others.
Some I gravitate away.
Some I gravitate towards.
All feel good.

Focus

I wanted to focus.
I was frustrated that I couldn't.
So frustrated that I couldn't.
I became scared.
I tried to force myself
By telling myself:
Focus focus focus.
You must focus.
And of course,
I didn't focus any more.
But when, I asked my mind, nicely -
Hey, is everyone in there okay with focusing?
They said, we're scared.
And we really don't want to.
Why they were scared I didn't ask.

I said,
I'd like to focus on this task for five minutes.
And I promise you we will be alright.
And I promise you I will check in with you after.
Would that be alright?
They said yes.
And for the first time.
I was able to work on my task for five minutes.
And I checked in on them.
And they were alright.
Taken care

Woke up yesterday

not excited for the day.
So many things I had to do.
No wonder I didn't want to put on my shoes.
But what if had to is get to?
Woke up today,
I get to play.
In meetings, conversations
Salivations while eatings
Relaxed.
The world is taken care of.
I can receive.
And even tease.

Petals

Pink petals falling,
and I'm here obsessing,
stressing about a calling.
But if I pause.

Isn't this just lovely.

Tapped

Connected to ground.
Tapped into source.

Life is unexpected and amazing.

To The Point

Getting to the point
where I respect myself enough
that I give myself permission
to take action for me,
not trying for others.

The Land

Why have I worked so hard to force something already
apparent?
A land I once saw as having no flowers,
I now love for being verdant green.

Annoy

The more someone annoys me,
the more I probably have to learn from them.

Above

Want to act from above?
Feed the love.
Clear the wants.
Forget the thoughts.

Nourishment

In what ways am I nourishing myself?
In what ways am I not nourishing myself?
What food am I eating to eat?
What food am I eating for the body?
What thoughts am I thinking to think?
And what thoughts am I thinking to make the body
happy?

Greatness

I wanted to be great.
And thought I needed to be extra for it.
So I pursued the extra
to no avail.
And so I let it go.
Accepted where I was.
And found that greatness
had been here all along.

Passively

You are welcome to be
wherever you are -
unemployed, in debt, without prospects.
Be there.
I didn't say be there passively.

Be there.
Experience it.
Embrace it.
Feel all of it.

And see what comes.
The situation may be
exactly what you need.

You get what you need.
And you can very well get what you want.

Responsibility

I take full responsibility for me.
Regardless of what happens in the external.
I take responsibility for the internal.

The Wave

I love riding the wave
that is given, and delighting
in the surprise
of how it might break.

Separateness

You want achievement.
You want a pedestal.
To show how good you are.
This requires others looking up at you.
Which means you're looking down at them.
That's separateness.
You want separateness.
Thats what your mind wants.
Not your heart.

Guess what.

It's not your mind
that makes you feel good.
Your heart makes you feel good.
And your heart loves connection.
Not separateness.

Love

What am I worried about besides love?
Why am I trying to do anything besides love?
Why am I trying to achieve anything besides love?
Oh I know.
I'm worried about not having love.
I'm trying to get love.
Love from other people.
Love for myself.
And that takes me away.
From offering love to others.
And to myself.

2024ish

"I am a lover of what is, not because I'm a spiritual person, but because it hurts when I argue with reality."

Byron Katie

Life

I feel so much love for myself.
I'm excited about life.

                    ... Didn't use to feel this way.

.

Fear

Fear

Fear is here.
Fear about not using my day.
Fear about not being my best.
All encompassing.
Restricting.
Taking time from me?
What can I do?
What can I do besides my art?
Even the taking the time to set up a new monitor.
Hurts my head.

Inhale

Inhale.
Exhale.
Time goes on.
Nothing you can do.

Inhale.
Exhale.
Time goes on.
Nothing you can do.
You can't slow it.
No no no no.

Inhale.
Exhale.
You can ride it.
This day comes.
And you get to experience it.
And the next comes.
You get to experience that too.
The contents.
Doesn't matter.

There is no good.
There is no bad.
You don't get to control.
Life is in the drivers drivers seat.
Life's deciding the destinations..

Inhale.
Exhale.
Times goes on.
So do you.
Time's always growing.

Your always growing.
Time's always expanding.
And so are you.

Inhale.
Exhale.

6 months into 30,
insecure Jerry
in my mind tells me I've done nothing with this time.
I need to do more.
I remind Jerry.
That life is about.
Feeling, growing
learning, laughing
Being wherever we are.

I

Who am I?
The filter.
The personality
The patterns, the loops
But am I not my personality.
I am also not the pattern.
I am the basic aliveness,
The basic consciousness,
Sitting in everyone.

Anxiety

Social anxiety.
Feaer. Fear.
Nervousness.
Wanting to really connect with
people I really want to connect with.
Don't worry about it.
Its okay if you don't.
Give yourself what you want from them.
Offer them what you want from them.
Laugh, smile, and be merry.
If that's what you feel.

If it happens, great.
If not, no matter.
There's no true connection.
Without being your true self.

Offer

Troubled?
Turn inward.
Have the strength.
to find peace in the chaos.
Once found.
Your eyes may then turn outwards.
Not to change.
But to offer.

Music

Wake up and see
what music resonates with me.
Is it calm, open, kind?
Is it loud, bangy, and encapsulating?
No need to change.
But notice.

Optimism

I realize that,
by forcing over-optimism,
by being out of reality
about my goals,
I have been dissociating
from a feeling of not
being worthy of them.
And in doing so,
ignoring reality.
And how can I work through reality if I can't see it?

Envision the goals.
Dream big.
Trust they can work out.
Be okay if they don't.
Be with reality.
Deal with the problems at hand.
And get there.

Given

Your time is given.
It is not necessarily for you to achieve.
It is not necessarily for you to do art.
It is for you.
When you wake up
The thought is not
what can I do today?
What should I use today for?
A thought could be,
how can I live today?
What brings my body joy today?
The days are here for you.

Today

Yesterday,
I woke up frantic.
Trying to find things to do
to bring me joy.
And nothing did.

Today.
I woke up rested,
thinking
what can I do for the those around me?
And I did many things
that ended up bringing me to joy.

Following the opening.
Want what you have.
And Let the river flow.

A child does not care
about who sees their art.
A child only cares
about the joy of the process of creating.

Following

When the mind
acts in service of the heart
the magic opens.
And that requires
letting go of control.
Letting go of leadership.
Relaxing the ego.
Forgetting perceptions.
And following.
And trusting.
Oh boy.

Skin

I'm realizing slowly
that I have not felt my life is for me.
It has been for others.
Trying to please, to be liked, to help.
To prove my existence to me through the approval of
others.
To prove my existence through betterman of the world.
To prove my existence through the impact on others.
To prove my existence through changing others.
Looking to others.
Not to me.

Me-ness

My me-ness
does not not extend past
what can flow through me.
I am at my best
when I am empty.

Positive

You get to live in positive anticipation.
In a state of looking forward to life.
Waking up happy, excited, energized.
And to do that.
You have to learn to love the road.
The ups, the downs.
You have to accept that it can be hard.
And you can be grateful for the downs.
And the downs show you the path up.
And to do that.
You have to accept that all experiences are experiences.
Positive and negative.
Sometimes you have pasta for dinner.
Sometimes you have pizza.
Sometimes you're happy.
Sometimes you're sad.
You can't control the road.
The road is already made for you.
Ride it, let go, and enjoy the glee.

Take

The only work I take
is to learn about the world
and grow myself.
So I can be myself
amidst the world.

Butterfly

The ego is a butterfly
trying to create the wind.

Only when its gives this up,
can it be itself.

And start pollinating.

Happiness*?*

Many people think we should be happy as often as
possible. Have as many peak experiences as possible.
Many Buddhists think we should move towards peace
and contentment.

Unhelpful

The ego is neither good nor bad.
When we follow the ego,
it is often unhelpful.

For the ego is lonely.
And does not see correctly.

Following it, we may lose connections.
We may try to be friends with people
for what they offer the external.
Not how they make us feel.
We may try to pursue goals,
for what they offer external.
Not for how they make us feel.
We may try to live in ways
so we can tell ourselves stories
about who we are that align with external.
Not how they make us feel.
Let go the ego.
Let go the external.
And follow the internal

Brave

Be brave enough to observe
what makes the internal feel good.
Be brave enough to follow
what makes the internal feel good.
And watch the richness of life grow.

Play

Today is a day.
You can do anything.
Why not play?

Overhead

The overhead of the pressure
of waking up
and taking action
to try and get
some external result,
be it an achievement
or a state of being
has not been of fun for me.
Let it go.
Stop trying.
Let it go.
And be.
Who knows where you'll go.
Fun is in mystery.

Discipline

Be disciplined.
Not in the actions
that the world tells you
you need to do so much of.

Be disciplined
in the actions
that foster
piece of mind.

Exercise.
Nature.
Nature.
Meditation.
Acceptance.
Compassion.

Trust

Whatever you achieve
Is in part because of source.
Because life happened to you.
And gave you the tools
to response to those circumstances
in your unique way.

So if you achieve
that means you can't really
take full credit.
If you achieve,
It's in part because of source.

So let go.
Trust.
Stop trying.
Let source unfold your path for you.
Maybe you achieve.
Maybe you won't.
But at least you'll be you.

And know -
that source does not care
whether you achieve or not.
Source sees your value.
Just for you.
100K

For a while I was sad

that in my first year of business
I barely made ends meet.
And I was sad
that I really only gotten most of business
because of one person.

And then I realized -
Hey, I made a 100K
in my first year
of starting a business.
And that's pretty good.
And hey also,
many businesses are initially started
By connections.

Change your perspective.
Change your energy.

A Gift

A gift enough
is respect and kindness.
There's no need to worry.
About not doing enough.
Or doing too much.

Channels

Opening the channels
letting energy move freely.
Letting myself be freely.
The jaw releases,
the breathe flows up.
And love is.
The self comes out.
Unrestricted.
Unregulated.
An animal whose been fenced in.
Balanced is learned.
Sitting in your seat.
Strong and compassionate.

Am

Who am I?
The filter?
The personality
The pattern, the loop?
But I am not my personality.
I am not the patterns.
I've learned in life.
I am the observer.
That sits in all of us.
One aliveness.
But if this is in everyone.
Is it really me?
I am this awareness
But I also am not this awareness.
Because who I am is distinctly
my personality. My filter.
Which is also not who I am not
So who am I?
Maybe the question is wrong.
Maybe there's not an I.
But ugh wait there must be...

Teenager

Life has never stopped
being as it was when you were a teenager,
when you were awaiting the world in front of you.
Joyful.
Without expectations.
Of what it should be.

Now you have expectations.

Bodies

Out of the mind.
Into the body.
Out of the stories.
Into the senses.
How good is this.

The Soup

The heart yearns for nature.
The heart yearns for animals.
It is not time for that yet.
Be in the city.
Be in the discomfort.
Learn from society, the soup.
It is okay.
The discomfort is okay.
We are alright.
The world spins on.
And the magic still happens.

Good Life

I have such a good life.
And I didn't have to create it.
I didn't have to do anything.
It was always here.
Waiting for me to see it.

Joy

Joy is the bird
that flies to you
of her own accord.

Warrior

Today I set out on my warriors path.
My sword- my sad heart,
allows me to wield compassion.

Aligned desires-
The compass that points me through the dark.
The mountain I intend to climb-
Attention to and alignment of my thoughts.

I will grow the thoughts
that love me.
I accept the thoughts that don't.
But tend to them I do not.

Thoughts may push me off my path.
I trust my sword to bring me back.

Discovery

The adventure is the not knowing.
Not knowing where we'll be.
Not knowing what we'll be.
Not knowing nothin.
So stop controlling.
The child's joy comes from discovering.

Courage

Courage is the power
to walk up to someone
and give what you want to receive.

I Live

Today, I live.
With death to my left.
And pie to my right.
Today, I live.

Where

I am finally free.
I know that the best way
to spend each day
is being exactly where I am.

Breathe

I've spent years
trying to figure out
how to Breathe.
Only to learn
it's the breath breathing me.

Peace

I know myself.
I sit in peace.
I did not know myself before.
And I was not in peace.
What kept me from peace?
Acting from fear.
Fear is still with me.
But it is not in the driver seat.

Regret

I do not regret
the years of not being me.
Contrast shows the way.

Oh My God

Oh my god oh my god oh my god.
My head is turning this morning
Trying to get out.
Trying to create something.
I feel tense in my jaw.
And pain in my chest.
Trying to create
the dream life -
travel, art, money, surfing-
that I've been told I should live.

Forgetting.

Free

To wake up
and to be
without worry
of what to do.
And just to be.

To wake up
and to be.
Be with me.
Without worry
of the world.
That's the free.

Want

What do I want?
What do I really really want?
Connection.
All of my peak experiences
are connection.
Connection with me.
Connection with others.
Connection with nature.
Connection with love.

Little Light

I'm not in the place I want to live.
I'm not in the work that I want to do.
I'm not with the community I want.
Part of me wants to run away.
But running has never gotten me far.
So I'm here.
I know I'm on the right path.
And I'm grateful for that.
A candle in the darkness.
You can focus on the dark.
And realize how dark it is.
Or you can focus on the
little bit of light.
And watch it grow and grow and grow.

Heart

Everywhere leads to nowhere.
So with everything you do,
you might as well to do with your heart.

Commitment

Now is not the time to hate.
As good as it feels.
As right as it seems.

I see where hate has gotten us.
And what hate has emboldened.
Hate can only strengthen more hate.

To lessen the hate in our country.
I want to lessen the hate in myself.

I used to want to ban those doing the hurting.
I now want to band with those hurt.
I used to want to undermine their stand.
I now just want to understand.

Sounds simplistic.
But what other way forward is there?

I believe in love, not hate.
I will offer love, not hate.

Exercise

Envision yourself
having gotten
all you wanted.
Feel yourself
having gotten
all you wanted.
Now feel.
That feeling.
For you.
In you.
For that feeling.
Is you.

The point here
isn't to get to that stuff.
It's for you to stop
using irrelevant stuff
as a means
to inhibiting
a relevant and deserved sensation.

Sadness

Sadness.
All-encompassing.
Consuming.
Engulfing.
Letting all the life out.
Leaving me an energyless blob.

Accepting.
Being with.
Not saying I should be.
Feeling something else.

Not saying I should be happy
allows space.
Space for observation.
Seeing the sadness
and being separate from it.

Gives space.
Space to think.
To do something that fills.
that soul a little bit.
Creates the space

to fill the soul a little more.
The next day.
Continuing on.

Suddenly the soul finds itself happy.

Thank you sadness.
For communicating something's off.

Thank you, me,
for listening.

Left

I have everything I have desired.
All there is left to do is give.

Letting Go

Letting go.
Letting go of the ego.
Letting go of need.
Embracing fullness.
In comes the desire for service.
Serving others.
Because it's what feels really good.
For ourselves.

Service

Sure, creating a social-good app sounds good.
But having the opportunity
to sit with people and serve?
Oh man that sounds satisfying.
Life feels purposeful with that thought.
Life feels relaxing with that thought.
Life feels like I can give up everything I'm trying to be
and be who I am with that thought.
Selfish.
Selfish service.

For

Yes, service is my why.
I am in service of others
But not for their sakes.
For my own.
I do not prove my worth
by changing them.
I am not here to change.
I am here to serve.

2025ish

"Fullness of life is on the other side of selfishness."

Jim Murphy

Attaching

You've been looking for a hobby.
Thinking that it will bring happiness.
And hobbies help with satisfaction at some level.
But you've been attaching to it.
Looking to it to deliver you.
Deliver you from wherever you are.
Enjoy where you are.
And soften into the doing
of what feels good
without expectation.
Be where you want to go.
Don't look for something to take you there.
And then go from there.

Choice

I could never figure out
which hobby I wanted to pursue.
And I lusted for a personal project
 to pour my energy into.
I tried a million different things.
And nothing stuck.
I never asked -
What fills my heart?
What has the most heart?
What is the greatest expression of my most authentic
self?
When I did,
the choice was clear.

Northstar

An internal sense of peace, joy, and appreciation
is the north star.
Observing the body's delight.
Be a follower and a truster
of you own experience.

Sky

Of the sky.
By the earth.

He Art

Earth
Heart
He Art

Navigating

Feelings are to be felt.
Good, bad, it doesn't matter.
All feelings are to be felt.
All are part of the experience.
The good ones, however,
are to be cultivated.
Are to be followed.
Are to be fed.
Open your doors to all.
And nourish only those.
That nourish you.

Smile

Smile, and smile big.
For it is time of connection.
And the world is beautiful.

Scary

The most scary thing for me
is to accept the passage of time.
The perceived loss of health.
The perceived loss of opportunity
to use the world as a means of
allowing myself to tell myself
the story that I want to tell myself
about myself
before I die.

So much fear.
About a story that doesn't matter.

            And what is aging?
The process of growing.
The process of expanding.
The process of coming home.
And the process of helping others
do the same.

Dieing

Dieing, no one looks at their trophies.
Dieing, we all look at our loved ones.

It is easy to forget what is important.

Connections are forever.

Trickster

The ego tricks you.
It tells you that achievement is more important than
connection.

Partners

The ego can be in the car.
It's great at filling up the tank.
And hitting the pedal.
Just don't give it the wheel.

You Go

From the heart you go.
All paths lead to nowhere.
So from the heart you go.
And the way it feels
Is the only thing that matters.

From the heart you go.
Fulfillment is from the heart.
From connection.
With yourself,
others,
and the world.

From the heart you go.

The Fires

Problem-solving life caused strife.
Following feelings is working out great.
Feeling peaceful, relaxed, and content -
A first priority.
Not by changing the external.
By opening into the fires of the internal.

Richness

The greatest richness
I could have been given
is wasting in stillness.

Calm

All paths are clear
with a calm mind
and a connected heart.

Grateful

My purpose has been revealed.
I am so grateful.
I got there
by following what fills me.
And then realizing that it also just so happens to be in
service of something greater than me.
Transcending is the self authentically is most exciting.

Back Again

Oh here the ego and mind go
with obsessing over achievement.
Needing to prove worth.
Oh baby we're back again.
It's their wish.
Not mine.
Hello friend.

Operating

This whole time
I've been operating
under the pretense
That if I do that
then I'll be happy.
If I find a career,
then I'll be happy.
If I find a hobby that brings me joy,
then I'll be happy.
If I find financial freedom,
then I'll be happy.

Oh boy.

And knowing this whole time
That happiness is here.
Joy is here.
Contentment is here.
Peace is here.
Satisfaction is here.
Connection is here.
And nothing needs to be done for it.
Knowing this.
And still trying to do for it.

Relax, open, soften,
and let it in.

Relax, open, and soften.

Breathe in.
Breathe out.

Relax
open
soften.

Breathe in.

Natural

Love exists.
It is the natural order.
Our mind creates a filter
that makes it hard to see.
Let go the mind.
Let go the filter.
Let go the stories.
And see the world,
like you did as a child.

In what ways am I still acting out of fear?
You're no longer overly fearful about not achieving.
Yet you still have many actions that come largely from
fear.
How can I start predominantly acting from love?

Thank you for your attention. 10% of proceeds will be donated to Jungle Keepers for their work protecting the Amazon.

Gurney can be reached by emailing beepboopgurney@gmail.com and including "Book Response" in the subject line.

It's a little embarrassing that, after 45 years of research and study, the best advice I can give people is to be a little kinder to each other.

Aldous Huxley

Made in the USA
Las Vegas, NV
13 April 2025

2fa60f5c-0e24-410b-bfea-0e8f8833e40cR02